D1274714

one time, one place

BOOKS BY EUDORA WELTY

A Curtain of Green
The Robber Bridegroom
The Wide Net
Delta Wedding
The Golden Apples
The Ponder Heart
The Bride of the Innisfallen
Losing Battles
One Time, One Place

one time, one place

Mississippi in the Depression | A Snapshot Album

eudora welty

RANDOM HOUSE

NEW YORK

94526

TR653
W44

Copyright © 1971 by Eudora Welty

All rights reserved under International and Pan-American
Copyright Conventions. Published in the United States by
Random House, Inc., New York, and simultaneously in Canada
by Random House of Canada Limited, Toronto.

Trade Edition: ISBN: 0-394-47308-6

Ltd. Edition: ISBN: 0-394-47322-1

Library of Congress Catalog Card Number: 73-162392

Manufactured in the United States of America

Design by Bernard Klein

6897

ACKNOWLEDGMENT

I wish to express my gratitude to the Mississippi Department of Archives and History, and its director, Dr. R. A. McLemore, for allowing me to reproduce these photographs. I am grateful as well to Mr. James F. Wooldridge, the custodian, for his patience and kindness. And I would like to thank particularly my old friend Miss Charlotte Capers, former director, under whose guidance the Department acquired and is now housing all of my photographs. Her long and affectionate interest in them encouraged me to assemble this book.

To Charlotte Capers

contents

Part Two

saturday

Part Three

sunday

Part Four

portraits

one time, one place

these photographs

these photographs are my present choices from several hundred I made in Mississippi when I had just come home from college and into the Depression. There were many of us, and of those, I was also among the many who found their first full-time jobs with the Works Progress Administration. As publicity agent, junior grade, for the State office, I was sent about over the eighty-two counties of Mississippi, visiting the newly opened farm-to-market roads or the new airfields hacked out of old cow pastures, interviewing a judge in some new juvenile court, riding along on a Bookmobile route and distributing books into open hands like the treasures they were, helping to put up booths in county fairs, and at night, in some country-town hotel room under a loud electric fan, writing the Projects up for the county weeklies to print if they found the space. In no time, I was taking a camera with me.

In snapping these pictures I was acting completely on my own, though I'm afraid it was on their time; they have nothing to do with the WPA. But the WPA gave me the chance to travel, to see widely and at close hand and really for the first time the nature of the place I'd been born into. And it gave me the blessing of showing me the real State of Mississippi, not the abstract state of the Depression.

The Depression, in fact, was not a noticeable phenomenon in the poorest state in the Union. In New York there had been the faceless breadlines; on Farish Street in my home town of Jackson, the proprietor of the My Blue Heaven Café had written on the glass of the front door with his own finger dipped in window polish:

The message was personal and particular. More than what is phenomenal, that strikes home. It happened to me everywhere I went, and I took these pictures.

Mine was a popular Kodak model one step more advanced than the Brownie. (Later on, I promoted myself to something better, but most of the pictures here were made with the first camera.) The local Standard Photo Company of Jackson developed my rolls of film, and I made myself a contact-print frame and printed at night in the kitchen when I was home. With good fortune, I secured an enlarger at second-hand from the State Highway Department, which went on the kitchen table. It had a single shutter-opening, and I timed exposures by a trial-and-error system of countdown.

This is not to apologize for these crudities, because I think what merit the pictures do have has nothing to do with how they were made: their merit lies entirely in their subject matter. I presume to put them into a book now because I feel that taken all together, they cannot help but amount to a record of a kind—a record of fact, putting together some of the elements of one time and one place. A better and less ignorant photographer would certainly have come up with better pictures, but not these pictures; for he could hardly have been as well positioned as I was, moving through the scene openly and yet invisibly because I was part of it, born into it, taken for granted.

Neither would a social-worker photographer have taken these same pictures. This book is offered, I should explain, not as a social document but as a family album—which is something both less and more, but unadorned. The pictures now seem to me to fall most naturally into the simple and self-evident categories about which I couldn't even at this distance make a mistake—the days of the week: workday; Saturday, for staying home and for excursions too; and Sunday.

The book is like an album as well in that the pictures all are snapshots. It will be evident that the majority of them were snapped without the awareness of the subjects or with only their peripheral awareness. These ought to be the best, but I'm not sure that they are. The snapshots made with people's awareness are, for the most part, just as unposed: I simply asked people if they would mind going on with what they were doing and letting me take a picture. I can't remember ever being met with a demurrer stronger than amusement. (The lady bootlegger, the one in the fedora with the drawn-back icepick, was only pretending to drive me away—it was a joke; she knew I hadn't come to turn her in.)

I asked for and received permission to attend the Holiness Church and take pictures during the service; they seated me on the front row of the congregation and forgot me; once the tambourines were sounded and the singing and dancing began, they wouldn't have noticed the unqualified presence of the Angel Gabriel. My ignorance about interior exposures under weak, naked light bulbs is to blame for the poor results, but I offer them anyway in the hope that a poor picture of Speaking in the Unknown Tongue is better than none at all. The pictures of the Bird Pageant—this was Baptist—were made at the invitation, and under the direction, of its originator, Maude Thompson; I would not have dared to interfere with the poses, and my regret is that I could not, without worse interfering with what was beautiful and original, have taken pictures during the Pageant itself.

Lastly, and for me they come first, I have included some snapshots that resulted in portraits: here the subjects were altogether knowing and they look back at the camera. The only one I knew beforehand was Ida M'Toy, a wonderful eccentric who for all her early and middle years had practiced as a midwife and in old age made a second life for herself as an old-clothes dealer; in the Depression she operated on a staggering scale. She wanted and expected her picture to be taken in the one and only pose that would let the world know that the leading citizens of Jackson had been ''born in this hand.''

It was with great dignity that many other portrait sitters

agreed to be photographed, for the reason, they explained, that this would be the first picture taken of them in their lives.

So I was able to give them something back, and though it might be that the picture would be to these poverty-marked men and women and children a sad souvenir, I am almost sure that it wasn't all sad to them, wasn't necessarily sad at all. Whatever you might think of those lives as symbols of a bad time, the human beings who were living them thought a good deal more of them than that. If I took picture after picture out of simple high spirits and the joy of being alive, the way I began, I can add that in my subjects I met often with the same high spirits, the same joy. Trouble, even to the point of disaster, has its pale, and these defiant things of the spirit repeatedly go beyond it, joy the same as courage.

In taking all these pictures, I was attended, I now know, by an angel—a presence of trust. In particular, the photographs of black persons by a white person may not testify soon again to such intimacy. It is trust that dates the pictures now, more than the vanished years.

And had I no shame as a white person for what message might lie in my pictures of black persons? No, I was too busy imagining myself into their lives to be open to any generalities. I wished no more to indict anybody, to prove or disprove anything by my pictures, than I would have wished to do harm to the people in them, or have expected any harm from them to come to me.

Perhaps I should openly admit here to an ironic fact. While I was very well positioned for taking these pictures, I was rather oddly equipped for doing it. I came from a stable, sheltered, relatively happy home that by the time of the Depression and the early death of my father (which happened to us in the same year) had become comfortably enough off by small-town Southern standards and according to our own quiet way of life. (One tragic thing about the poor in Mississippi is how little money it did take here to gain the things that mattered.) I was equipped with a good liberal arts education (in Mississippi, Wisconsin, and New York) for which my parents had sacrificed. I was bright in my studies, and when at the age of twenty-one I returned home from the Columbia Graduate School of Business—prepared, I thought, to earn my living—of the ways of life in the world I knew absolutely nothing at all. I didn't even know this. My complete innocence was the last thing I would have suspected of myself. Anyway, I was fit to be amazed.

The camera I focused in front of me may have been a shy person's protection, in which I see no harm. It was an eye, though—not quite mine, but a quicker and an unblinking one— and it couldn't see pain where it looked, or give any, though neither could it catch effervescence, color, transience, kindness, or what was not there. It was what I used, at any rate, and like any tool, it used me.

It was after I got home, had made my prints in the kitchen and dried them overnight and looked at them in the morning by myself, that I began to see objectively what I had there.

When a heroic face like that of the woman in the buttoned sweater—who I think must come first in this book—looks back at me from her picture, what I respond to now, just as I did the first time, is not the Depression, not the Black, not the South, not even the perennially sorry state of the whole world, but the story of her life in her face. And though I did not take these pictures to prove anything, I think they most assuredly do show something—which is to make a far better claim for them. Her face to me is full of meaning more truthful and more terrible and, I think, more noble than any generalization about people could have prepared me for or could describe for me now. I learned from my own pictures, one by one, and had to; for I think we are the breakers of our own hearts.

I learned quickly enough when to click the shutter, but what I was becoming aware of more slowly was a story-writer's truth: the thing to wait on, to reach there in time for, is the moment in which people reveal themselves. You have to be ready, in yourself; you have to know the moment when you see it. The human face and the human body are eloquent in themselves, and stubborn and wayward, and a snapshot is a moment's glimpse (as a story may be a long look, a growing contemplation) into what never stops moving, never ceases to express for itself something of our common feeling. Every feeling waits upon its gesture. Then when it does come, how unpredictable it turns out to be, after all.

We come to terms as well as we can with our lifelong exposure to the world, and we use whatever devices we may need to survive. But eventually, of course, our knowledge depends upon the living relationship between what we see going on and ourselves. If exposure is essential, still more so is the reflection. Insight doesn't happen often on the click of the moment, like a lucky snapshot, but comes in its own time and more slowly and from nowhere but within. The sharpest recognition is surely that which is charged with sympathy as well as with shock—it is a form of human vision. And that is of course a gift. We struggle through any pain or darkness in nothing but the hope that we may receive it, and through any term of work in the prayer to keep it.

In my own case, a fuller awareness of what I needed to find out about people and their lives had to be sought for through another way, through writing stories. But away off one day up in Tishomingo County, I knew this, anyway: that my wish, indeed my continuing passion, would be not to point the finger in judgment but to part a curtain, that invisible shadow that falls between people, the veil of indifference to each other's presence, each other's wonder, each other's human plight.

Jackson, March, 1971

8

Part One

workday

Chopping in the field | WARREN COUNTY

Cotton gin | HINDS COUNTY

Boiling pot | HINDS COUNTY

Making cane syrup | MADISON COUNTY

Tomato-packers' recess | COPIAH COUNTRY

Making cane syrup | MADISON COUNTY

Washwoman | JACKSON

*Washwomen carrying
the clothes* |
YALOBUSHA COUNTY

94526

Schoolchildren meeting a visitor | JACKSON

Nurse at home | HINDS COUNTY

Blind weaver on the WPA

Schoolteacher on Friday afternoon | HINDS COUNTY

Part Two

saturday

Saturday Off | JACKSON

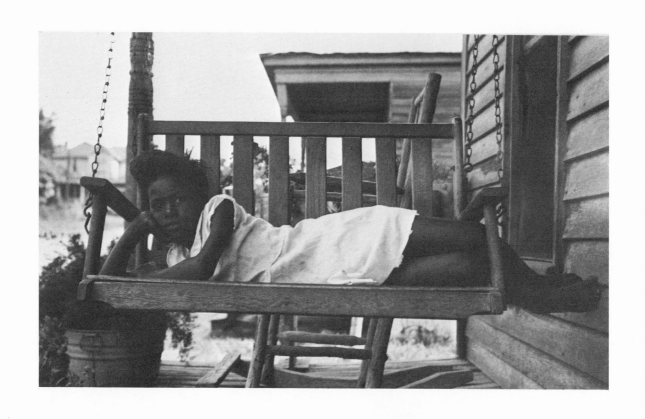

Boy with his kite | JACKSON

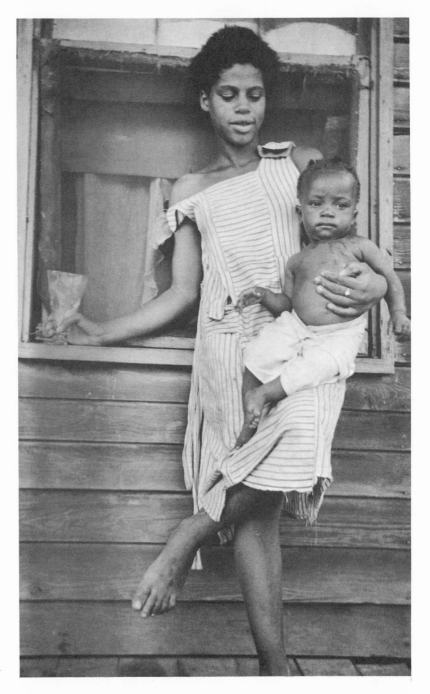

Coke | JACKSON

Hairdressing queue | HINDS COUNTY

Front yard | YAZOO COUNTY

With a dog | UTICA

With the baby | HINDS COUNTY

With a chum | MADISON COUNTY

Home | CLAIBORNE COUNTY

36

Home | MISSISSIPPI RIVER, NEAR GRAND GULF

Home | JACKSON

Fisherman and his boys throwing knives at a target |

Home with bottle-trees, sometimes said to trap evil spirits
that might try to get in the house | SIMPSON COUNTY

Home, ghost river town | RODNEY

Home after high water | RODNEY

Home abandoned | OLD NATCHEZ TRACE, NEAR CLINTON

To play dolls | JACKSON

To find plums
COPIAH COUNTY

To all go to town | HINDS COUNTY

Hamlet	RODNEY
Village	HERMANVILLE
Saturday in town	GRENADA

Town in a store window | CANTON

The store | UTICA

Window shopping | GRENADA

Crossing the pavement | UTICA

Strollers | GRENADA

Tall story | UTICA

Farmers in town |

CRYSTAL SPRINGS

Store front | CANTON

In the bag | CANTON

If it rains | JACKSON

Confederate veterans meeting in the park | JACKSON

Making a date for Saturday night |

Making a date | GRENADA

The fortune-teller's house | JACKSON

The bootlegger's house. Pretending to drive away customers with an icepick | HINDS COUNTY

Political speaking | PONTOTOC

Political speech | TUPELO

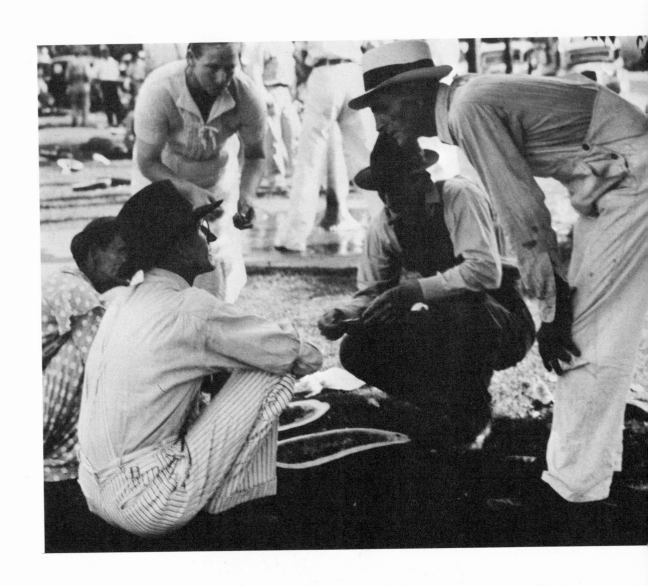

Watermelon on the courthouse grounds | PONTOTOC

SMITH COUNTY

RALEIGH
POST No. 97

TAYLORSVILLE
POST No. 85

MIZE
POST No. 101

County float, State Fair parade | JACKSON

Church float, State Fair parade | JACKSON

Club float, Negro State Fair parade | JACKSON

Free Gate, State Fair | JACKSON

Beggar at the Fair gate, with jigging dolls |

Hypnotist, State Fair | JACKSON

Sideshow, State Fair | JACKSON

The Rides, State Fair | JACKSON

Sideshow wonders, State Fair | JACKSON

Too far to walk it |

Part Three

sunday

Sunday School. Holiness Church | JACKSON

Preacher and leaders of Holiness Church | JACKSON

Make a joyful noise unto the Lord. Holiness Church | JACKSON

Speaking in the Unknown Tongue. Holiness Church |

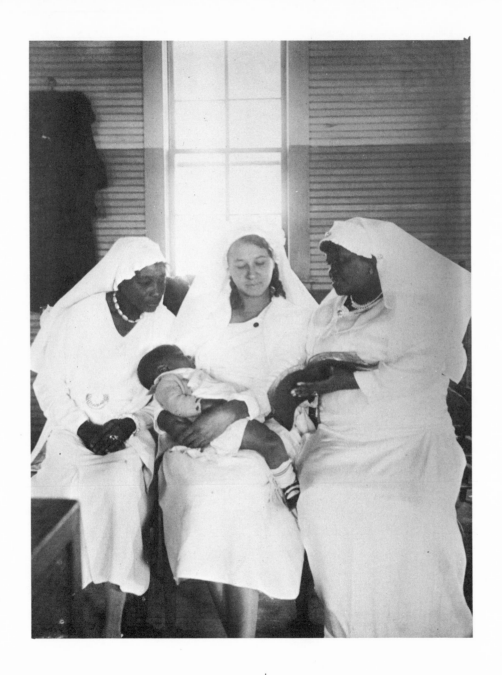

Baby Holiness member. Holiness Church |

Baptist deacon | JACKSON

Members of a Pageant of Birds, Farish Street Baptist Church |

Bird Pageant costumes | JACKSON

Baby Bluebird, Bird Pageant |

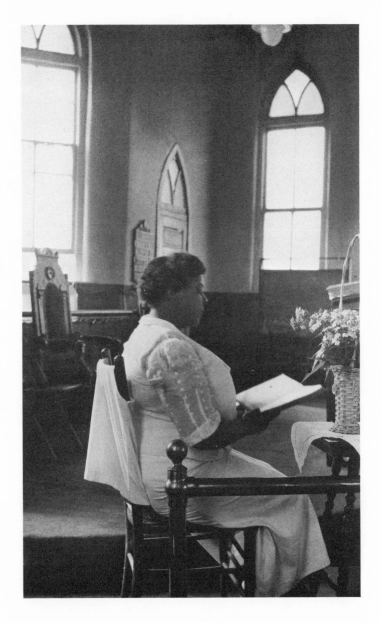

*Author and director of the Bird Pageant. "To raise money to
buy not a new piano but a better one."* | JACKSON   91

Country church | NEAR OLD WASHINGTON

Country church | NEAR RODNEY

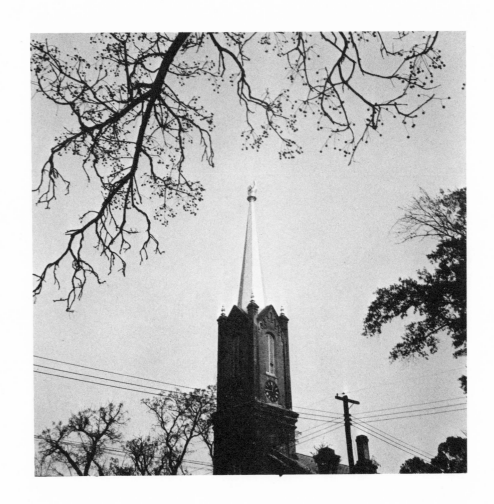

Church in Port Gibson

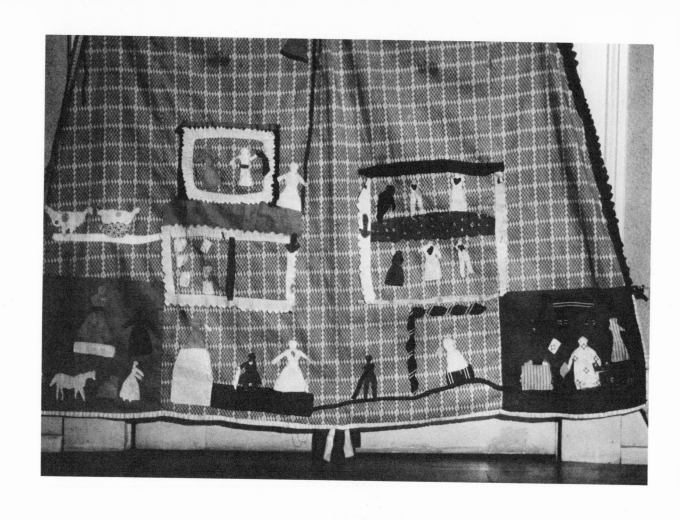

A slave's apron showing souls in progress to Heaven or Hell

YALOBUSHA COUNTY

Carrying the ice for
Sunday dinner | NEAR BOLTON

Part Four

portraits

Wild flowers | HINDS COUNTY

Ida M'Toy, retired midwife |

Ida M'Toy

Delegate. Governor's Mansion | JACKSON

Storekeeper | RANKIN COUNTY

Hat, fan, and quilts |

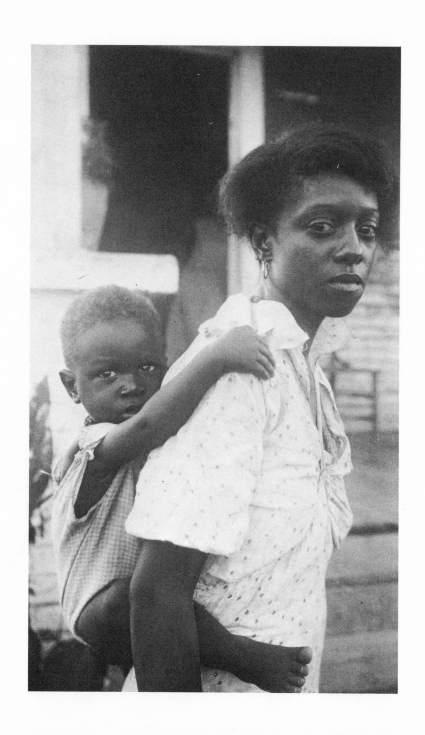

Mother and child
HINDS COUNTY

A village pet | CLAIBORNE COUNTY

Yard man | CLINTON

Mother and child | HINDS COUNTY

Four sisters | HINDS COUNTY

Home by dark | YALOBUSHA COUNTY

eudora welty was born in Jackson, Mississippi, which is still her home. She was educated locally and at Mississippi State College for Women, the University of Wisconsin, and the Columbia University Graduate School of Business, where she learned to type. Her short stories have appeared in *The Southern Review, Atlantic Monthly, Harper's Bazaar, The New Yorker,* and other magazines. She has lectured at a number of colleges, has held the William Allan Neilson professorship at Smith, the Lucy Donnelly Fellowship at Bryn Mawr, and was a lecturer at the Conference of American Studies at Cambridge University. She has worked under grants from the Rockefeller and Merrill Foundations and the National Institute of Arts and Letters, and has held a Guggenheim Fellowship. She has been given honorary degrees from Smith, the University of Wisconsin, Western College for Women, and Millsaps College in Jackson. She also received the M. Carey Thomas Award from Bryn Mawr, the Brandeis Medal of Achievement, and the Hollins Medal; her novel *The Ponder Heart* was awarded the Howells Medal for Fiction by the American Academy of Arts and Letters.